THE GROWTH OF A FLOWER WITH A TORN STEM

Sonder's Serenity

For: my sister, two brothers, and dad

Table of Contents

Addiction

See I find myself with an obsession

Trying new things

Taking in the lessons

I fill up the vile and start injecting

The anger, sadness, hurt

Slice into my veins

See this feeling alone would drive any sane man away but I bask in it

Eyes rolled back

I'm possessed

See my hand starts to itch when I get stressed

I didn't choose this lane

This lane chose me I'm blessed

With every situation and hurt, came the need to decompress

See these things have been boiling

Heating up this dangerous mixture

Maybe a dash of fear of rejection, and some of those feelings from

when I was 11 and it finally became clear to me that I was emotionally

neglected

All my life i been stressing

Hand itching

Trying to find a new way to twist my words

Decompressing

Locking myself in my mind

That's the only place I feel free to stretch in

Basking in my lesson

Slouched over from the pain

Maybe I'm an addict, maybe I'm in insane

But my words will paint a picture

They'll scream, they'll cry

They'll comfort you, might get you high

See this is the island I built

In this raging ocean Just me and my words

Mixed with the nerve to see clearly, every emotion

Not for what I want it to be

Reality is truly depressing

But I'll face it

Hand itches

I find myself decompressing

This is an addiction not an obsession

I am an addict with a pen.

Growing pains

My mistakes cloud my mind and weigh on my shoulders

The whispers of what should have been done

Ring in my ears constantly

I fall deeper and deeper down into myself

Scared to make the next move

Then I shatter

The glass foundation gives way

Leaving me aching all over

From the impact of what I had done

I have to look it in the face

This monster I call mistake

I take it and consume it

It coats my insides with many things

Hurt,

Regret,

Anxiety,

But most of all understanding

Then I rebuild

And do it Again,

And again,

Till I have the right pieces

To build the foundation

To this tower I call myself

Loosing braincells

I stare at the backs of my eyelids

As the thoughts fill up my head

Loud but quiet

Full but empty

Taking up so much space, these thoughts create a void

And I feel my brain deteriorate.

With each retched thought,

A weight gets placed on one spot

Latching on like a virus

Refusing to let go

And it grows

And grows

Until it becomes to heavy to bear

And that piece of my brain crumbles

Joining the other unearthed thoughts

In the pointless void

I can't pinpoint when it started

The slow death of my brain

But over the years the thoughts have become white noise

And I've become tone death to its maliciousness

Feeling the void grow

But never knowing which cord to pull

To loosen the knot,

One could argue that I should dive in

And discover

But I'll stay on this island Surrounded by darkness

Because the idea of drowning is much scarier then

The sensation of my bones begging to hollow out

I lose these pieces of myself every day

But I embrace it

Wondering if it's just my cocoon

Hoping I'll become a butterfly

Praying it's more than an empty husk.

My body

From the blemishes that scatter across the back of my shoulder blades,
wrap around and kiss the center of my chest
To the stretch marks on my thighs that seem to be a simple reminder of
how I've grown
The discoloration that makes up my skin, like it simply cannot make up
its mind.
This body is mine
You took one look at it
And decided that you wanted it
No matter the blemishes
Or the marks
Or the discoloration
You still found me beautiful
And the fact you found me beautiful
Was enough

Chapter 1
FIRST LOVE

her.

Your words enter my ears like a sweet melody

I feel them travel down and enter my stomach Pooling there with

warmth leaving traces of your love behind

The warmth spreads

Easing the ice of my aching wounds

The ice of my heart

Till it consumes me

Then I melt

Becoming a puddle that slips through your fingers, leaving nothing but

my heart behind

I surround your feet,

I'm this puddle of emotions

Yet I don't feel weak

Or alone

I bask in your love that surrounds me

I cradle your words close to my chest

I'm finally at peace

Knowing you my love

Will take my heart Build it up

And watch it grow a new me

As you hum a melody that is the key to the lock around my soul I watch

as you set me free

I watch myself being loved by you

My lover's sickness

There's a weight on my chest that you placed unknowingly

I take it and label it as my own

I know I did no wrong,

yet it still feels as tho it's my fault

That it's me

That I'm the problem

But I know I did nothing

And I know you

I know how you act when u feel negative emotions

Ur walls of thorns shoot up

You ball yourself up

And allow yourself to be a product of your environment

You feed every ugly emotion

And I watch as the thorns multiply even though it hurts

I still try desperately to climb over them and hold you

For every prickle of every

Thorn

I know deep down you do not mean it

You don't mean to create this distance with this wall

I accept you for who u are

And where u are in life

Just as you did to me

I need not be your knight in shining amour

For that is not my calling

I sit and I wait patiently

For you to allow my love entry

Into your domain

To be healed

It's crazy how the quality of life can improve so much

To always want them there

To always have someone to think about

To have the smallest moments mean so much

To be able to genuinely smile

To feel safe

And secure

To have someone that makes wanna

believe

Believe in yourself

Believe in others Believe in god

Because there's no way such a beautiful soul wasn't crafted

The taste of sweetness from her words

The warm feeling of her laugh

The butterflies my stomach gets from her smile

The way my insides feel like molasses from three simple words

I love you

And the euphoria I get from not doubting those words is unexplainable

Like a bear hug on a cold day

I hold those words close

Caressing them into unimaginable things

And I'll never doubt that I'm the luckiest girl on earth

To have the opportunity to love

And to be loved

To have found my soulmate at such a young age

To understand the feelings that some truly dream about

Damn, it feels good to have you

Dry tornado

I see you

Here with me finally

In this moment finally

I'm so scared that if I blink

You'll disappear

Holding on to the aspirations of your existence

I cling to you like I'm in the desert

And you're my last drink of water

Like you're my reason for living

Breathing

And yet

It's not enough to speak u into existence Isn't it pathetic?

How I rid myself of my dignity

And bare my full chest to you

Even though, you're not here with me, in this moment?

I rid myself of all other worldly senses

And leave me defenseless to you as predictable as a hurricane I take that damage

I tell myself it's worth it

For that's the price you pay for this addicting warmth

This oozing overflowing feeling inside

The ultimate gamble

To feel your love and love you back

Or to add to our collection of cuts where we bleed gold

And cry ourselves dry about our misery

The greatest love

My best love wasn't truly love

But addiction

To lose oneself in another Is the greatest feat

To be able to escape reality

To have my vision covered with the good

And bad of her

To be able to give myself

Willingly

But every high has a comedown

Every movie has an end

Every love doesn't last

One must answer

When reality calls

Over the sound of my emotions crashing

Over the sound of her

Time stops for no man

And I'd rather drop my heart

Then my time.

Mixed emotions

I knew
Letting myself go into the unknown
Had consequences
Yet I chose to do it anyway
I let you cut open my chest
And take a peek at my insides
I let you take a crack
At the intricate puzzle
Full of mushy organs,
Cold and dark despair,
Emptied hollowed-out bones,
And the faintest glimmer of light.
I let you take a crack at arranging me
For the best
Not knowing that you'd take advantage
And try to build me in your image
To get me to worship the very ground you walk on

To get me to abandon everything I've known
And have yet to know,
To get me used
To the uncomfortable feeling
Of my insides being out of place.
Never mind if I die,
All that mattered
Was that I loved you
The way you wanted
The way you intended me to
All that mattered
Was that I was
Who you built me to be.

Mirror

I miss the emotions that used to rush through me

The comfort of knowing I was still human

The pain that reminded me I was still alive

What am I without these things?

And an empty husk?

A nameless face?

I gave you myself

And lost the best parts of me.

You took the one thing that made me human

And screamed monster

But am I not what you created?

Am I not your offspring

Am I not a visual of your own reflection?

Are you discrediting your art

That you painted on my insides?

That you engraved into my heart?

That you coaxed me to believe?

Do you not like your work?

Does it not make u smile to see

The ruins of me.

Will i disappear?

I am a ghost

An empty shell of the person

I used to be I surround myself with people

In hopes for normalcy

Time passes me by

People come and go

And start to blur

They become hollow shells with no faces

They become ghosts like me

And I cover myself

Hoping they can't smell me rotting

From the inside out

My soul was a blank canvas

Pristine and white, simply beautiful

As I grew old enough to walk

People began painting

Marking

Claiming my soul as their own

Reaching inside of the caverns of my body

And ruining my once clean soul

And when I got old enough to talk

To understand the words they were saying

As they painted on my soul and called it their own

One thing became clear

They painted on mine

Just as someone had once painted on theirs

And the ones before them

They did not understand

The damage because

They had abandoned theirs

Claiming it as dirty, ruined, unloveable

But the worst artist of them all

Cried malice, hearts bled desire and want

Smiled In loneliness and laughed in evil

Their words became chants

As their brush ran across my rough canvas

Spewing sewage

And none of these artists stayed to claim their work

Leaving after realizing, that my canvas was like theirs

I cover my ears

squeezing my eyes shut

Humming melodies to escape from their words

And their brushes

Until one day, one person removed my hands from my ears

And cried, beautiful

They took my canvas and handed me a brush of my own

Telling me to claim my art, my soul

And so I painted

And for once

I see my canvas as something more

Then what had been painted on I saw me.

So close but yet so far...

I'm here, in this moment

Floating by

Empty smiles

Empty laughs

Empty mind

You'll laugh at my antics

At the show, I put on

To hide the sludge of misery I feel inside

The thick overgrown sludge

Screaming for help

Hidden behind my eyes

You'll love and you'll touch and enjoy my presence

Never realizing

It's less than the essence of myself

Fading

My voice has been stolen

My throat has run dry

My screams fall on dead ears I scream

And I scream

I am here

I am important I exist

But to no avail

The blurred faces keep moving

These unknown souls

Intertwined around each other

Lick their teeth and laugh

Ignoring my despair

Ignoring my existence

Ignoring my importance

And I watch as I fade

I watch as my very existence itself

Disappears

Chapter 2

HEARTBREAK AND NEW CONNECTIONS

What if?

I lay awake wondering

What could have been

If I'd just changed one decision in my life If I'd taken another road,

Would I be this miserable?

Would I be this lonely?

Would I be this broken?

What if I'd been strong enough

To speak my mind,

To say no?

To find my voice which had been stolen from me?

Yet I sit here

In a puddle of my own disgust and self-hatred

Knowing I'm no better than my abuser

Hearing my soul screams bounce around my hollowed insides

Cold,

Empty

Alone.

Is this my karma?

Is this my destiny?

Is this my punishment?

The undying sadness

The undying loneliness
Watching myself crumble
From the inside out
And being able to do nothing
But weep at the destruction
Of me.

Not truly mine

Eyes that sparkle

Mind of a million things at once

And nothing at all

A safe place

In a home that isn't mine

Knowing I'll soon be kicked out

I'll stay regardless

Finding her smile to be worth it

And her beauty to be bountiful

Her laugh comforts my aches

And her banter softens the ice

In my bones

Her encouragement holds me up

And her company brings me peace

Is it foolish

To not want to tie something so beautiful down

To not want to capture it

But to watch it grow

And flourish

To admire its beauty is enough

To ease the ache in my heart

To watch her eyes sparkle to the end of my days

Would be enough

I'd find myself being selfish

To want her to myself

To not be able to share such a beautiful presence

Such a beautiful soul

Strong But fragile

A passion that isn't fierce

Or overwhelming

But calm and stagnant

The rhythmic sound of the waves

Matches the beat of my heart

As such soothes me enough

To be comfortable

In my skin

In my passion

For you.

Stay

Is it wrong to ask you to stay?

Even though I was the one who pushed you away

Is it wrong of me to want your presence

The same one that broke me

The same one that drained my veins

The same one that made me this way.

Is it wrong for me to want u here

Even though your not mine

Even though the future is unclear

To want your warmth

To melt the icebergs in my bloodstream

Your laugh

Your smile

Just one more day

One more word

One more laugh

One more moment

Stay here with me

And make memories

That won't last just a day

But an eternity Even though a life without you is near

Even though I know

This rocking boat Is destined to flip I'll choose to be selfish

Please Just Stay.

Just Stay.

MINE.

Your eyelashes are dusted with gold
And your eyes full of pools of crystallized honey
That becomes a gooey mess with one glance at me,
Overflows
And sticks to my heart
I'd curl up in your insides
And make my home there
I watch myself fall into your eyes
And the comfort they bring
Pure beauty
Is what they'd scream
If they'd get the opportunity
To discover your warmth
I like to think
My body heat feels nice
That my love oozes and coats ur insides
And that you'd never get
My sickly sweet smell
Out of your walls
I'll claim this home as my own
For it is to precious
To do anything but preserve
To do anything but love
To do anything but make my own
It is mine and mine alone.

She is....

If I could compare her to something I'd compare her to the breeze

The untamable, mesmerizing breeze

No real pattern

No real blueprint

It is itself in its very being

Kissing noses and breathing life into kites

Carrying wishes on its back into the unknown

And dancing with the leaves on the trees

I'd also compare her to the harsh winds

The ones that push and pull the tide

Shift trees at their roots

And can whistle and scream at the wrongdoings of the inhabitants of

earth

In the still of night, I yearn for her light feathery

Touch

The feeling of freedom she brings

Peace and comfort she blows

Pushing my very being to and fro

Never once tipping me

But reminding me

That I too am free.

In my window

Those eyes stare at me with childlike wonder

shining with curiosity

At the bruising, dents and shards

Which shivered and told ghost stories of another

They reach in despite my warnings

My words fall on deaf ears

As the sickly beautiful shards reflect off the light

They reach in and gasp as the cruelty, selfishness, and suffering dance

around their fingers

Their eyes prickle with accusation

And their finger shifts with agitation

As they scream

Evil.

I never allowed myself to love you

And I'm glad I didn't

I'm glad I kept my heart under lock and key

Another blank face with empty promises and a beautiful soul

Reaching out to feel warmth from another being

Looking to be whole

And when I denied my heart

Not for selfish reasons but

Because the ache of my wounds was to raw

To bear another touching such a sore spot

The ghost turned into a demon

Screaming in agony

Spoiled and selfish

Mad it didn't get its way

It's face turned dark

And it's skin cold

As the old demeanor fell away

I watch as this beautiful soul

Blamed me for protecting myself

For not being quick to allow them to love

And love them back.

Stranger

Voice so smooth

It slides over the windows of the walls

That contains my emotions

Is this an enemy?

Shall I dare resist this devil?

With eyelashes that curl reaching for the stars

Outlining beautiful orbs that seem to turn into planets

If I look hard enough

Haunted planets

Late at night, they seem gather

And whisper the secrets of the galaxies

A smile that would melt the coldest bones

And yet

I still falter,

From having seen the most beautiful specimens

Turn rotten in front of my eyes

Natures food chain

Another serpent

Has made its way into my garden

Dusting itself with the pollen from my flowers

Scenting itself with the bark and overgrown grass of my life

Dipping in and out making itself a new

When it presented itself to me I cradled it

Thinking it nothing more than a living being

As it entangled itself around my bones

And when it saw the opportunity

It's body recoiled

And it's newfound skin was shed

As it leaped and bit

Not to eat or because it felt threatened

But to inject the poison into my veins

Hoping for the chance to rob my sanity

Hoping we'd become just the same

As this serpent didn't want to be alone

And I in this garden

Was just too pretty to leave alone.

Glass half full

How can i describe

The absence of oneself

The feeling of being hollow

Never knowing who you are or what you want

I wonder what enticed my soul

To leave it's caverns

Cold and barren

The walls weep and groan

As it's warmth is gone

Leaving them ridged

And tight

I feel them close around themselves

As my chest moves in and out

With the rhythmic sound of their sorrow

Who knew

It could mean so much

Empty vessels

Making their way through a crowd

Blindly

Seeking fulfillment

They fill each other with different forms

Of fancy emptiness

And cry in short-lived joy

Till they realize they've been filled with nothing

And began their journey

Once again

Moving blindly through the vast crowd

Seeking to be fulfilled

Seeking to be whole

feelings?

If you were to ask me how I felt

I could describe

The feeling of my ribs twisting around another

The feeling of my heart reaching out into the abyss

The feeling of my soul caving in

Scared to show its face to another

I'd describe the lump in my throat

That appears only to taunt my voice

Breaking it apart

Piece By Piece But what good would it do

To pour my despair onto another?

To have someone bare this burden

That I carry?

Is it not my responsibility to carry it alone?

Is that not the choice I made

By leaving my chest open to the world?

So if you were to ask me how I felt,

I'd grit my teeth

And smile

And say

"I'm fine, how about you?"

Ghost lovers

Long smiles

Wandering eyes

Blank emotions

Phantom touches

To be loved or to not be loved

The ultimate gamble in this world

What is such a soul-seeking

Comfort, pain, experience, excitement, passion?

Is its mind empty?

Does it know the consequences of its actions

The act of taking in to many

The act of applying ghosts on its back

The act of covering wounds with people

The act of reaching out for an easy fix

The drug of ghost lovers.

My old friend

The tightness in my chest is oh-so-familiar

My lungs is the soil

And my stolen breath is the water

The very thing I need to survive

Fertilizes the thing that makes me not want to

I feel my muscles constrict

And my teeth grind

As I bear this weight

This grief

This loneliness

The very thing I've been desperately running away from

Surrounding myself with random strangers

Filling the hole inside my chest

Hoping to keep it expanded

Hoping to stop my insides from crushing themselves

Hoping that eventually,

I'd be able to breathe on my own

But one by one

The faces become unfamiliar

Their words became foreign

And I once again am alone

Chapter 3
FULFILLMENT

Lost and found

I learned that

For one to find themselves

They must lose themselves first.

How can one find,

Something that is not lost?

So I'll let the mucky feelings

Fill my chest

I'll embrace the fact that

No matter how I feel

My eyes seem to remain dry

I'll embrace me

Even though it's hard

Even though I always feel less than normal

It is me

Titanic

How can I be meant for greatness?

What makes me so special?

This battered skin that hugs my frame

Never feels like my own Am I insane?

How does one feel like themselves and know who they are at the same

time?

A constant cycle of my soul-breaking

And being put together in a new way

Hoping to be stronger

But now

I fear that my soul cannot be saved

What if it's to broken to repair?

As I lay in my bed at night

Drowning in despair

While only one thing runs through my head

Who am I?

self hatered

The feelings crash around in my chest

Mixed with the well-deserved hunger

My body screams

Care for me

Do better

Love me

But the empty feeling is almost comforting

I've found my long-lost friend

I'll allow it to consume me

And fill me whole with its vision of peace

It's own vision of sanity

It's own vision of happiness

I'll let it hold the wheel even if just for a little while because I cannot

bear to open my eyes

To look at reality

To accept the pain

Disappointment

And selfishness of others

And the scariest thing

The main reason I'd refuse to open my eyes

Is the fear

That I'm no better than the ones who hurt me.

Daydreamer

I hold my head high

Some say it's in the clouds

I Call it an empty void

Nevertheless,

I keep my eyes sparkling

And my smile glimmering

I convince myself I'm okay

I push and persevere

I'm strong

An enigma

I'm a dream

All these things

And I want to be Nothing

I want to be one with the air

I want to lay with the stars

I want the weight of my body to be left behind

I'm exhausted

I want to be free

Solitude

Who knew that I'd waste away

My feelings crumbling to dust

And my heart shriveling in disgust

With itself

Isn't it pathetic

To lock such a large amount of love away

Isn't it sad

That I'd rather be alone

That I'd rather deal with me being lonely

Then deal with another soul again

Purgetory

The feeling of having so much love to give

The feeling of purity

And my heart thumping against my chest

The feeling of the blood rushing down my veins

Catering to the knots in my stomach

All these things pile

And pile

Afraid I'd combust

Afraid I'd drown in my longing for another

Now I stand envious

Of her

How easily it was for her to like me

How willingly she poured into me

Not knowing that I

Once like her

Had poured into another empty vessel

Leaving myself with nothing

I tried to hold her close

My greed overtaking me

Telling myself different

But no matter how she poured

Fast or slow

My vessel remained empty

My blood still felt cold

And my heart calm

How desperately I wanted to love her

How desperately I wanted to be able to return her emotions

But I now know that I have nothing to give

Nothing to pour into those sweet nothings

Nothing to warm her bones

I took one look at what she poured

And I returned it

Even though the thought of me forever being empty

Haunted my very core.

Poignant

My face sags from the weight of the past

My body bent with the burdens of others

I watch as people pass me by

Never moving to scream for help

Never bothering to acknowledge

The agonizing pain of existing

Refusing to look at myself in the mirror

Refusing to acknowledge my need for help

Who can help Someone who's cursed

To be in pain for eternity?

Who can help Me?

Ocean floor

Going through the motions

Rolling with the tide

The salt of the water

Stings against my aging soul

Running in this water is pointless

Straining my bones just to end up

Two inches from where I started

I don't know when I stopped moving

When I stopped trying

I just know

I'll let this water push me

Till I reach the point where my feet can't touch the bottom

Leaving me with only two choices

Sink or swim.

tired

An exhaustion that's made its home in my bones

Seeping through my pores and latching itself to my skeletal system

Turing into a form of gravity

Hoping I'll become one with the earth

Hoping I'll give into its weight

And as tempting as it is

A chance to take a never-ending break

I know that this weight

Although painful

Difficult

And malicious will make me stronger

Than I've ever been before

wilted

A frail flower planted by a riverbank

Soft mud fertilizes her and runs through her veins

But when the cold harsh winters hit

It's the very thing that keeps her alive

Thats keeps her stuck in place

But when spring comes

And melts the ice away

She Droops her towards the water

Hoping to be saved

Or hoping to be washed away

Sometimes her beauty will fall upon a random wanderer

They'll see the droop in her stem lifelessness in her petals

And Scream

She needs to be saved

Shall they take her up roots and all

And plant her anew?

Will they be helping her or destroying her moving her away from her home

Was she not built to withstand these conditions?

Just because her mud was not to their liking

Or her posture not very straight

But yet that she was all she knew

And without it, she might go insane

Embodyment

What determines my worth?

Is it the brown skin that wraps my frame

Gliding over bones that make hips

And fat that makes my chest and thighs?

Is my sensuality?

Is it my smile that some claim as perfect

Or my lips that can be mistaken for pillows

Or my brown eyes that say everything and nothing at all.

Is this what makes me worthy?

Or maybe it's my big heart

That seems to ache from old wounds

Whenever it feels to much

Or my mind which crackles with new ideas

Some good some bad

The home to my dreams

Ambitions

And also my nightmares. Is it my soul?

The air in my frame

That seems to glow at random moments

And hide away from potential threats

Or old memories

What can my worth be amounted to?

A decent life where I grow old with pets and die in my own comfort?

Or a life of love where I can grow and learn with another

Or maybe nothing.

Whose place is it to judge my worth?

Who can say I'm worth more or less

Why do I have to be worth anything?

Isn't every life precious

Should I not be entitled to decent treatment?

How can I know what I'm worthy of

If I cannot seem to determine my worth?

Ache

This ache seems to appear
Whenever I feel an ounce of happiness Is there any relief?
Not painful but yet
Enough pressure on my heart to make its presence known Is this a form of guilt?
How can something linked to emotions
Take such a strong physical form is this normal?
Am I normal?
Or am I just insane?
Insane from the past faces
And traumas
And things no man can explain
Or maybe I'm perfect
No not perfect,
Good enough
Good enough to be loved
Good enough to be enjoyed
Good enough to be happy
Maybe this ache is a reminder
Of my growth
Maybe this ache symbolizes
The stretching of my heart
To care about someone once more
As it cries in fear
Of being hurt again
But it cannot help itself
As it's to big
To care only for itself alone.

Reciprocation

I tend to love the wrong people

Not the type of love where I want their hand in mine

Or where I steal kisses underneath the moon

But the type of love where id take the marrow from my bones

To fill their empty ones

The type where id sit on the sidelines and wait patiently

To be tapped into the game of their life

The type where id give and expect nothing in return

But no matter how much I care

Or try to love these people

I am always a second thought

I am always left with empty bones

That I hang up infront of my heart

Letting them rattle in the wind

Full of nothing but empty dreams and willingness to do anything for

another

I try to be patient and kind

Id never expect the same thing in return

But id appreciate an ounce of sincerity

An ounce of importance

Something to show that the seed that I planted

Is fruitful

And yet all I get is the reminder that I am alone

When I seek shelter from the storms I get rained on

Knowing I would've opened my home to them

Knowing id never allow them to get sick

Knowing the love I give is far from basic

It is complicated and messy

Unspoken words hang heavy

As I do these things silently

So I fall into myself

Remaining nice but not friendly

Because in this cruel world

The simple act of loving another Is craved

But I have to many empty bones

I think its time

I love myself Unapologetically

As my newfound wind chimes play the most beautiful melody

Telling ghost stories of another

Over it

I used to crave one's company

But now it feels like

It's the last thing I want

I find more comfort in my own demons

Than the wicked ways of another being

I think its finally time

I allow myself to be alone Even if it destroys me.

desert

The dry crisp air

Makes the dryness of my lips ache

Sweet to the taste but yet

It suffocates my lungs

The wetness of my eyes

Contrasts against the dryness filling my frame

The fall blues

That's what I call this

Everything about this season

Contrasts my warm body

The sharp winds

That come and go

Make me feel my own embrace

And I remember that I too

Am warm

I am reminded

That I too Am alive.

Velocity

I cannot stand chaos

The calm rumble of my thoughts

And sparks of ideas

As I grow and discover

The way my nerves seem to burst and explode

Seeping in and becoming my very being itself

This chaos that I have inside

Doesn't help the ins and out of life

Sometimes i don't know how I don't implode

Yet the still-ness of night

And the clouds moving even though they look

As if they settled and nestled into their newfound home

Goes to show

That everything can be nothing at all

Everything changes, moves and grows

Even when it doesn't show.

Grief

My chest

Comforts a comfortable ache

One that holds pieces of you

In slivers of muted memories

I wonder if it would be better if I didn't feel this pain at all

Would the guilt not consume my very being?

Would I forget you?

This pain is a reminder that you lived

And that I loved you

I love you

This pain is the result of the cruelties of life

The same ones that snatched your soul

And set you free from the flesh prison

That we call body

My heart weeps as I continue to live

I wonder how I haven't drowned in my sorrow

But then I remember

That the very love that causes this ache

Makes me believe Someday

I'll be able to hold this unrequited love

And be comfortable in my pain for you

In my love for you

I don't know if you'll receive it

I'll release it into the universe

In hope it reaches you

Gluttony

I feel everything

And nothing at all

Selfish they scream

For not making a coat of my skin

Or using my bones to kindle the fire of their life

I am a wretched person

Who hides behind my morals

And reasoning

Never knowing what choice is correct

But to you I seem so sure

You want me to abandon myself

To reassure

Even though your belly is full

Even though your limbs warm

Even though the fire never burns out

You want me to love you at the expense of me

You want me to give myself to you

As you had given yourself to someone else

You want me to continue this cycle

Shortsighted

Narrow-minded

Blinded by the pleasures of life

I am selfish

Because I like my skin as is

And I like my bones in place

I am selfish

For loving myself as I am I'll never apologize

And I don't care to be forgiven
I'll be selfish
I'll be all the things you deem me to be
As long as it keeps my treasures safe
From your greed.

Giver

The giver has a full supply Candies, pickles, chips Oh my

In the back you can find books, phones

Shoes and more

Hidden in nooks and crooks, look and find

Everything you could imagine is stored right there inside!

See the giver has been in this business for years

Giving and giving

He knows no fear!

Why didn't they tell him

There's no such thing as an endless supply?

The giver has less but he still has some!

A pickle maybe

Or some chips , and a piece of gum…

Wait never mind the giver has no more

But wait let's see what he has in store

For what is a giver that cannot give

Let's see,

All this giver has to offer Is his tears

From eyes that hold no self-importance

But no matter

The giver will give

Until the giver is no more

This is his curse, his nature

He has surely matured!

See

The giver will give to anything that is not his own

Maybe, his neck, his leg, or even his phone!

The giver knows no boundaries or fear

The giver will always be near

Only there when he is needed, doesn't linger or meddle

He always gives the utmost quality

Then leaves, never giving himself time to settle.

Never mind what he sees or hears See the giver only has one goal, one

purpose He has to fill never-ending hunger.

Oh no the giver is no more

But I'm sure he has inspired

Who shall be the giver next

Since this one is retired?

Hurt people hurt people

The smoothness of my skin was tantalizing

You envied it

Believing ur scars were less than

Believing they made you

As though the roughness of the scar became your

shield

That you often hide behind hugging ur knees

Wondering Why me?

The rage inside

From the simple unfairness of life

Can be consuming

I watch as the maliciousness ignites

As u strike

Wanting us to be just alike

Wanting me to feel ur pain

Because carrying that burden alone

Can drive one insane the loneliest feeling creeps in and settles at night

Making a home out of your bones

And nestling next to your veins

And somewhere down the line

You found comfort in the pain

You wanted me to relate to you

As if the uniqueness of my walls wasn't enough

My new house smell

Caused u to derail

Screaming

Scratching

Throwing

Anything to knock me down to the comfort of your bones

Hurt people hurt people

After all.

What is love?

Is it hidden looks

Or bright smiles Is it empty?

Is it whole?

Is it a real thing at all?

See to me love used to mean abandonment,

Leaving everything including common sense behind

The ultimate act leaving myself unguarded

But Being pushed and pulled with the tide I grew sea sick

And wanted nothing but to hide away inside

But I've grown cried, And now?

Do I have a real answer to this question?

Ill never know

Ive accepted the fact that

I am love

And love is me

Hand in hand we grow

If I had to describe it though?

Id say its an adjustment,

The willingness to pick a person

Not for any good reason

Other than the fact that they exist

In the same moment and time

When my hands get to full

Love will be the discovery

That all I had to do was shift my pinky

A little to the right to hold so much more.

Love is bright and new

It is dull and boring

It is loud, it is quiet

Fulfilling and painful

Love I guess is a chameleon

Existing in everything

Breathing in millions

Love is not only from hooded eyes smiles

Or unrecognized butterflies

Ive found that when I breathe

I am loved

When I see

I am loved

I am loved because I exist

I can discover, discuss and adjust

Love is freedom

Unapologetic

And robust

So no matter how many times I feel unloved

Or a muck

Ill adjust

And I must trust that

I am love and love is me

noir

Today I used the last of my body wash

Now to any normal person this isn't some great feat

But to me

Having grown up in a house of 6

Using the last of the body wash could be considered an ultimate crime

See I was raised to be considerate but stingy

Like adding a little water to the soap when things got heavy

I was raised to make my best better

And to always prepare for the worst

This is the start of my generational curse

It funny how when I made it to middle school It was nothing like I rehearsed

Different customs and ideals It really was the worst

I wasn't considered black enough Having never seen poetic Justice,

Nor listening to rap

Having being feed books, freethinking,

I never thought that everything I knew would be considered crap

Its funny

I really had a time in my life where I wished I wasn't black

As if the blackness of my skin amounted to

Weather I did or didn't like chicken

I started to feel like a piece of me was missing

Internal racism is an unspoken trap

By the time I outgrew these ideals,

Childish games and very unappealing feels

I began to use my blackness as a mask

Its funny how many will take a straight faced black woman For an unapproachable brat I laugh as they cower in fear

Simply because I am black

Knowing that underneath all that

Im scared of guns, I actually like puns

And social settings is the only time I find myself enjoying rap

What about this thing that all of a sudden everyone started glorifying
as a crown?

This thick, unruly thing that refuses to be tied down

Yet when I cover it

I find people looking down, turning up their noses

Their smiles find their way upside down

Black women must accept and hold themselves to a higher standard

But what if I unleash the beast?

The coils seem to defy gravity, just begging to be released

Heavy is the head that wears the crown

As I have grown into my blackness though

I feel a sense of peace

I just hope that one day

Black women will find a release

There will always be a new anchor

There will always be new police

There will always be a new body wash

So why do I feel such unease?

This is a few of many generational curses I hope to defeat

self perseverance

I find it interesting

To feel the stress of the future seep out of my bones

To watch myself evolve

To be able to smile with no pain

No Tomorrow

No yesterday

Just today, right here, right now, in this moment I exist

Not for money

Or love

Or the basics I exist for me

The blood in my veins pumps MY heart

And my heart alone

I'm happy

I can't remember the last time I warmed my own bones

Who knew I was so comfortable?

Cup half empty

Big balls of emotions sit in my chest

Never moving or identifying itself

Sometimes it feels like there's nothing left

But in the dead of night

They bounce around my chest

Reminding me of the ache that never left

When you overpour a cup

Does the new water replace the rest?

Or does it bounce off the back of its brothers

Getting lost in the abyss?

Does it cry in agony

Being removed from its home

Until it dries up having died

Now that it's not in a place where it can be strong?

See I want to flourish

I want to bloom

But I'm afraid I'm not in the right place

Big ball of emotions

Taking up so much space

Hiding in plain sight

Just out of reach

Enticing newfound emotions

Every time I try and sleep

Ominously waiting

To steal my ability to breathe.

My chest once again

Shivers and quakes

Underneath this weight

That seems to only get heavier the longer it rests

Each breath becomes harder

Each thought louder How does one take a break?

How can I escape myself?

Cursed with life long sorrows

Only if I could borrow

A breath of fresh air

Something light and airy

To contrast the cold dark despair

Im forced to swallow every night

Choking on the pain

What do I gain?

Except the right to my own life Maybe it'd be easier if I didn't wallow but

see This pain is old

And every year it gets harder and harder to swallow

Tears prick my eyes

Enticed by old memories or

The thought of once-clear skies

I know it's just a moment,

But it only takes an average human 2 minutes to drown

I still fall into this pit even though I'm never looking down

I wish for peace and clarity

A moment of sanity

So I can unravel this knot that seems to find new ways to tangle

And elope

With my insides

Enticing me into a downward spiral

As I sit and laugh and smile

Clearly in denial

That I'm still rotting from the inside out.

I count my days like blessings

Never knowing when I'll fall into the ground

Never knowing when my life will be turned upside down I'm blessed

But even the most fortunate

Couldn't operate underneath this stress I'm a mess

I want the best for myself yet

I can't seem to stop looking back

How can I let go of the past

If that's all I have left

How can I move forward without forgetting you

You're face is blurry on my day to day

But at night I can still hear your laugh

Feel your aura

And I once again fall into this trap

Of looking back

Stuck in the past because "the good ole days" weren't good until they

didn't last

Wanting to grasp

A moment

Engrave it in my brain

Make it last

Because that's the only place you can exist now

Being exiled from this earth

I pick through those memories

Like a lost and found

Wondering which new coat would fit me now

See I've grown bigger

Stronger

But yet when I look back

All I can do is frown

Haunted by what should've been done

But nothing can be done now

See you're in the ground

And I'm stuck looking around

Grasping at straws

Faces unblurr

Was that really your favorite song?

Did we even truly get along?

Bittersweet

Hoping I'm not going about this wrong

Wanting to keep u in my heart forever

But I don't think it's that strong

How can I move past this? It's really been to long,

I miss you Fuck

Contact the Author:

Instagram: sere.nesonderr

X: ithurtslovingu